Admiralty Office United Kingdom government

Uniform Regulations for Officers of the Fleet

1891

Admiralty Office United Kingdom government

Uniform Regulations for Officers of the Fleet
1891

ISBN/EAN: 9783742852939

Manufactured in Europe, USA, Canada, Australia, Japa

Cover: Foto ©ninafisch / pixelio.de

Manufactured and distributed by brebook publishing software (www.brebook.com)

Admiralty Office United Kingdom government

Uniform Regulations for Officers of the Fleet

ADMIRALTY,

10th October 1891

In pursuance of Her Majesty's pleasure, the following are the descriptions of the Uniform to be worn by the Officers of the Royal Navy.

By command of their Lordships,

Evan Macgregor

CONTENTS.

	PAGE.
Extracts from the Queen's Regulations and Admiralty Instructions	5
Officers' uniform, description	8
Uniform of Officers, Royal Naval Reserve...	20
Uniform of Officers, Royal Indian Marine...	20
General instructions...	21
Dresses, and occasions on which they are to be worn	23
Tailor patterns	27
Coloured plates of uniforms	30

UNIFORM REGULATIONS

FOR

OFFICERS OF THE FLEET.

EXTRACTS FROM THE QUEEN'S REGULATIONS AND ADMIRALTY INSTRUCTIONS.

FROM CHAP. II.—CEREMONIES AND DISTINCTIONS.

§XV.—UNIFORM.

116. The officers, men, and boys of Her Majesty's Fleet and the Royal Marines shall wear such uniform as the Admiralty shall, in pursuance of Her Majesty's pleasure, from time to time direct.

2. The descriptions of the various articles of uniform are specified in the uniform regulations, and will be published from time to time in the Navy List.

The prescribed patterns are to be strictly adhered to.

When to be worn.

117. Every officer, from the time of his joining the fleet, squadron, or ship to which he shall be appointed, to that of his being removed from it, shall wear the uniform established for his rank, except when he shall have leave from the Admiralty or the senior officer to be absent from his duty, or as hereinafter provided.

Plain clothes.

2. Permission may be given to the officers to wear plain clothes on ordinary leave; but at reviews, public balls, or entertainments given by naval or military authorities, by civil functionaries, or by military messes at ports at which their ships may be lying, officers are to wear the uniform of their rank, as prescribed for the various occasions specified under "Dresses, and occasions on which they are to be worn," and no deviations are to be authorised without special authority previously obtained from the Admiralty.

Subordinate officers.

3. Subordinate officers when on ordinary leave are to wear the uniform of their ranks; but permission may be granted to them to wear plain clothes when going into the country, or to ride, shoot, play cricket, or for exercise.

Foreign ports.

4. In foreign ports great discretion should be exercised in allowing officers to appear out of uniform, as in such cases they can have no right to expect to be recognised as British officers.

Royal Marines.

5. Officers of the Royal Marines are to wear their full dress on the occasions when half dress and frock coat with epaulettes dress are worn.

Officers on retired and reserved lists.

118. Officers on the retired and reserved lists, whose names appear on the list of the Navy, are permitted to wear the uniform of their respective ranks on state and other occasions of ceremony.

§ XVIII.—Wearing Decorations and Medals.

Decorations and medals, how to be worn.

128. Her Majesty approves of the following regulations as to wearing decorations and medals :—

a. Decorations and medals are to be worn with 'full' dress.

b. They are to be worn on the left breast in a horizontal line, suspended from a single bar placed in a line about one inch below the point of the shoulder, but no part of the bar or buckle is to be seen.

c. The ribbon is not to exceed one inch in length, unless the number of clasps require it to be longer.

d. The buckles attached to the ribbons of the third class of the orders of the Bath and of St. Michael and St. George, being part of the decoration, are to be shown half-way between the upper and lower edges of the ribbon.

e. When the decorations and medals, on account of their number, cannot be suspended from the bar so as to be fully seen, they are to overlap.

f. Medals will be worn in the order of the dates on which they were conferred, the first decoration or medal obtained being placed farthest from the shoulder.

g. The following is the order of the arrangement :—

    I. British decorations.*
    II. British medals.†
    III. Foreign decorations.
    IV. Foreign medals.

h. The medal for long service and good conduct is to be worn after all British orders and medals.

i. Chief gunners, chief boatswains, and chief carpenters, warrant officers, and chief officers of coast guard, who have been awarded the good conduct medal prior to their promotion, are to wear it in accordance with the regulations of this article.

j. Medals awarded by a society for bravery in saving human life, if specially authorised to be worn, are to be worn on the right breast.

---

* The Queen's jubilee medal will be worn after British decorations.
† The badges of the order of St. John of Jerusalem in England will be worn after British medals.

2. Officers who are Knights Grand Cross of orders may wear the broad ribbon of the order, or the broad ribbons of the orders to which they belong, with full dress and ball dress uniforms only, the ribbon or ribbons being worn over the waistcoat. Knights Commanders will wear the ribbon of the order, or the ribbons of the orders to which they belong, inside the collar of the coat, the badge being suspended two inches below the lower edge of the collar.

3. On similar occasions, officers who may be members and honorary associates of the order of the Hospital of St. John of Jerusalem in England, are to wear the badges of the order.

4. Stars of orders and ribbons of decorations and medals are to be worn with the frock coat with epaulettes dress; ribbons of decorations and medals will be worn with frock coat dress and undress. These ribbons are to be sewn plain on to the cloth of the coat or jacket, without intervals, and must be the full size, and half an inch in length. They are not to be made to overlap, as in the case of medals, but when there is not sufficient room to wear the ribbons in one row, they are to be worn in two rows, clear of the lappel, the lower row being arranged directly under the upper. In such cases the ribbon of a Knight Grand Cross, or Knight Commander of any order, is not to be worn, the ribbon of the Companion of the order being substituted.

5. Stars of orders are never to be worn with the undress coat, or jacket.

6. An officer who is a Knight Grand Cross of an order may wear the star of the order with all uniforms except undress, mess dress, and mess undress.

7. An officer who is a Knight Commander of an order is to wear the star and badge of the order with all uniforms on which epaulettes are worn.

*8. Miniature decorations and medals are only to be worn on the undress tail coat and jacket; they are not to be worn under the lappel, but, when their number requires it, the bar is to extend over the lappel.

9. Stars of orders, and miniature decorations and medals, are authorised to be worn in evening dress (plain clothes) in the presence of members of the Royal Family, or of Viceroys and Governors-General, and on public and official occasions.

10. Retired officers are authorised to wear stars of orders, and miniature decorations and medals, in evening dress on all public and official occasions.

11. In all cases the bar for the suspension of decorations and medals is to be provided at the expense of the wearer. It may be of any metal or material, and of any pattern consistent with the above instructions, provided the bar and the buckle are wholly concealed by the ribbons.

* The miniature decorations here referred to, only include those worn in a line with the medals, such as C.B.; C.M.G.; C.S.I.; V.C.; D.S.O.; &c., &c.

OFFICERS UNIFORM.

INDEX.

1. *Rank* and *branch* distinctions.
2. Full dress coat.
3. Collar of full dress coat.
4. Cuffs.
5. Undress tail coat.
6. Frock coat.
7. Undress coat.
8. Jacket.
9. Trousers.
10. Waistcoats.
11. Epaulettes.
12. Shoulder straps.
13. Buttons.
14. { Swords, scabbards, and sword knot. Dirk.
15. Sword belts.
16. Aiguillettes, and sash.
17. Cocked hat.
18. Cap and cover.
19. Cap badges.
20. Helmet and puggaree.
21. Foul weather hat.
22. Neckties, and comforter.
23. Gloves.
24. Boots, and shoes.
25. Gaiters.
26. Great coat.
27. Waterproof coat and cape.
28. Boat cloak.

Dress of Chaplains (page).

1.—RANK AND BRANCH DISTINCTIONS.

(1.) All coats are the same for commissioned officers, except full dress coats of Chief Gunners, Chief Boatswains, and Chief Carpenters.

(2.) The principal indication of rank is the stripes on the sleeves, and, when not worn there, on the shoulder straps.

(3.) Branches are distinguished as follows :—

Military	By the circle on the upper row of lace.	
Medical	" scarlet cloth.	In conjunction with the stripes.
Accountant	" white "	
Engineer	" purple "	
Naval Instructor	" light blue "	

(4.) Nine sizes of gold lace are used, viz. :—(Plate X.)

Ranks.	Size of Lace on					
	Cocked hat and shoulder straps.	Trousers.	Collar.	Flaps on the skirt.	Slash on sleeves.	Stripes on sleeves.
Flag Officers ...	2 inches.	1¾ inch.	1¼ inch. ¾ "	1¼ inch.	1 inch.	1¾ inch. ½ "
Captains and Commanders ...	—	1½ "	1¼ " ½ "	1½ "	¾ "	½ "
Lieutenants ...	} — {	1¼ "	1 " ½ "	1 "	½ "	½ " ¼ "
Sub-Lieutenants		—				
Warrant Officers, over 10 years' seniority	—	—	—	—	—	¼ "

Unless otherwise specified, officers of the civil branch wear the same lace as the corresponding ranks of the military branch.

(5.) The uniform of Commodore, 1st Class, is the same as Rear-Admiral, except the epaulettes and devices on shoulder-straps.

(6.) The uniform of Commodore, 2nd Class, is the same as Captain, except the cocked hat, full dress sword belt and scabbard, cuffs, and shoulder straps.

(7.) Officers of the navigating branch will wear the same uniform as Captains, Commanders, and Lieutenants, according to rank, except as stated under epaulette devices.

2.—FULL DRESS COAT. (PLATES I. AND IX.)

For all Commissioned Officers, except Chief Gunners, Chief Boatswains, and Chief Carpenters.—Blue cloth, double breasted, eight buttons in each row, three inches apart across the breast, the skirt to begin at one-fifth the circumference from the front edge, and lined with white kerseymere; one button at the bottom of each plait, and two in the waist seam behind. Pointed blue flaps on skirt and three buttons under them.

For Flag Officers, and Commodores, 1st Class.—Flaps on skirt laced all round with 1¾ inch lace. A row of 1 inch lace to encircle the hip buttons and form a point above them on the seam.

For Commodores, 2nd Class, and Captains.—Flaps on skirt laced all round with 1½ inch lace. A row of 1 inch lace to encircle the hip buttons and form a point above them on the seam.

For Commanders.—Flaps on skirt laced all round with 1¼ inch lace.

For Lieutenants and Sub-Lieutenants.—Flaps on skirt laced all round with 1 inch lace.

For Chief Gunners, Chief Boatswains, and Chief Carpenters, and Warrant Officers.—Blue cloth, double-breasted, eight buttons in each row, to button the four lower buttons, fall-down collar, round cuffs, with three buttons and notched holes of blue twist thereon; pointed flaps with notched holes of blue twist and buttons under them to correspond; three buttons in the fold of the plait of the skirt; the skirt to begin at one-fifth the circumference from the front edge.

See Tailor Pattern of Full Dress Coat **A**, *page 27.*

3.—COLLAR OF THE FULL DRESS COAT (PLATE XI.)

For all Commissioned Officers, except Chief Gunners, Chief Boatswains, and Chief Carpenters.—White cloth, the front edges slightly sloped, and fitted with a black silk tongue to cover the space between them; fastened at the bottom with one hook-and-eye.

To be trimmed with gold lace according to rank, namely :—

Flag Officers.—1½ inch top and front edges, ⅜ inch lower edge.

Captains and Commanders.—1¼ inch top and front edges, ¼ inch lower edge.

Lieutenants and Sub-Lieutenants.—1 inch top and front edges, ¼ inch lower edge.

Not less than ⅛ inch of white to show between the upper and the lower lace. If necessary, the lower lace may be partly on the coat.

10

4.—CUFFS OF THE FULL DRESS COAT. (Plates XII. and XIII.)

For all Commissioned Officers, except Chief Gunners, Chief Boatswains, and Chief Carpenters.—Blue cuffs, with a white pointed slash with 3 buttons, and rows of distinction lace according to rank; the dimensions of the slash are: 7 inches high at the points, 6½ inches at the seam, and 2¾ inches wide at the centre. The outside edge of the slash bound with gold lace according to rank, namely :—

Flag Officers and Commodore, 1st Class	... ...	1 inch wide.
Commodore, 2nd Class, Captains and Commanders	...	¾ ,, ,,
Lieutenants and Sub-Lieutenants	... ...	½ ,, ,,

Rows of distinction lace :—

For Flag Officers, and Commodore, 1st Class.—A band of 1¾ inch lace round the cuffs, with rows of ⅝ of an inch distinction lace round the sleeve above the cuff, according to rank, viz. :—

Admiral of the Fleet	4 rows	The upper row to form a circle 2 inches in diameter, in the centre of the upper sleeve.
Admiral	3 ,,	
Vice-Admiral	2 ,,	
Rear-Admiral, and Commodore, 1st Class	1 ,,	

For Commodore, 2nd Class.—A band of 1¾ inch lace round the cuffs, and a circle 1¾ inch in diameter formed of half-inch distinction lace above it.

For—

Captains	... 4 rows	of ½ inch lace.
Commanders ...	... 3 ,,	
Lieutenants over 8 years' seniority ...	... 2 ,,	of ½ inch lace with a row of ¼ inch lace between them.
Lieutenants under 8 years' seniority	... 2 ,,	of ½ inch lace.
Sub-Lieutenant	... 1 row	
Chief Gunners and Chief Boatswains	... 1 ,,	
Gunners and Boatswains over 10 years' seniority	... 1 ,,	of ¼ inch lace.

The upper row to form a circle 1¾ inch in diameter in the middle of the sleeve.

For Officers of the civil branch.—The cuffs will have the same number of rows as those of officers of the corresponding ranks in the military branch, but the upper row will be straight instead of being formed into a circle, and the space between the rows will be of coloured cloth according to branch.

Assistant Paymasters of 6 years' seniority ...	1 row of ¼ inch lace above 1 row of ⅛ inch lace.
Engineers under 6 years' seniority	

The space between each row of distinction lace to be one-quarter-of-an-inch.

5.—UNDRESS TAIL COAT. (Plates II. and IX.)

For all Commissioned Officers (except Chief Gunners, Chief Boatswains, and Chief Carpenters), Midshipmen over 18 years of age, and Clerks.—Blue cloth, double-breasted, six button holes in each row, four in the turn and two below, padded turn-down collar; pointed flaps with three notched holes of black twist, and buttons under; one button at the bottom of each plait, and two in the waist seam behind. Round cuffs, the sleeves laced, as in full dress, omitting the slash. Shoulders fitted for epaulettes.

See Tailor Pattern of Undress Tail Coat **B**, page 27.

For Midshipmen.—The collar to have on each side a white turnback of 2 inches, with a notched hole of white twist, 1¾ inch long, and a corresponding button. Three buttons on each cuff, with corresponding notched holes of black twist.

For Clerks.—The cuffs the same as Midshipmen, but with one row of ¼ of an inch wide white cloth.

6.—FROCK COAT. (Plate III.)

For all Officers, except—

> Midshipmen,
> Naval Cadets,
> Assistant Clerks.

Blue cloth, double breasted, with padded turn-down collar; cut for six buttons, but to have five buttons on each breast, to button four buttons; the width of lappel to be 3 inches at fourth button, tapering to 2½ inches at waist seam; two buttons on the hips, with side edges in plait of skirt extending half way down the skirt, with a button at bottom of each side edge; for Officers 5 feet 9 inches in height, length of coat 38 inches, with a proportionate variation for difference in height.* Lining, black silk. Hook for sword belt.

Round cuffs, sleeves laced as in full dress, omitting the slash.

Shoulders fitted for epaulettes; the fittings covered with blue cloth.

See Tailor Pattern of Frock Coat **C,** *page* 27.

7.—UNDRESS COAT. (Plate IV.)

For all Officers.—Blue cloth, with padded turn-down collar; the length to be sufficient to cover the hips; double breasted, with 5 holes and buttons at equal distance on each side, to button four. Pockets, without flaps, at the sides, in a line with the lower button, and one outside left breast pocket. An opening 5 inches long at the bottom of each side seam.

Round cuffs, the sleeves laced as in full dress, omitting the slash.

Midshipmen will wear the same distinction marks on the collar as described in No. 5.

Naval Cadets will wear, on each side of the collar, a button hole of white twist, 1¾ inch long, with a corresponding button.

Clerks and Assistant Clerks will wear, round each cuff, one row of ¼ of an inch wide white cloth.

See Tailor Pattern of Undress Coat **D,** *page* 28.

WHITE UNDRESS COAT. (Plate IV.)

White drill, single breasted, stand collar, with hook and eye at neck, five buttons up the front, and an opening at bottom of each side seam, five inches long. A patched pocket on each breast, without flaps. Shoulders fitted for shoulder-straps, if required.

Midshipmen and Naval Cadets are to have the same distinction marks on the collar of the white undress coat as on the blue, and there is to be an eyelet hole in the collar for the button.

---

* The proportionate variation in length of skirt, for each inch of difference in height, is ½ of an inch.

8.—JACKET. (Plate V.)

For all Officers, except—
    Midshipmen,
    Naval Cadets,
    Clerks,
    Assistant Clerks.

Blue cloth, double breasted, six button holes in each row, four in the turn and two below, padded turn-down collar; slightly roached over the hips, with a rounded peak behind; two pockets, with welts, at the sides.

Round cuffs, the sleeves laced as in full dress, omitting the slash.

See Tailor Pattern of Jacket **E**, *Page 28.*

For Midshipmen and Naval Cadets.—Blue cloth, single breasted, with 7 buttons; 3 notched holes of black twist on each cuff with buttons to correspond; a stand-up collar with a hook and eye, and with the white turnback and button-hole, as described in No. 5 and No. 7. When worn it is always to be hooked at the top.

For Clerks and Assistant Clerks.—The same as for Midshipmen, but with a plain turn-down collar, 3 button holes in the turn and four below. One row of $\frac{1}{4}$ of an inch wide white cloth round each cuff.

White Jacket. (Plate V.)

For all Officers.—White linen, and of the same shape as the blue jacket for commissioned officers, but with a roll collar; to be worn linked with two No. 2 size buttons connected by a ring.

Shoulders fitted for straps if required.

9.—TROWSERS. (Plate VIII.)

Laced.—
    Blue cloth, with a gold stripe down the outside seam—
        $1\frac{3}{4}$ inch broad for Officers of Flag Rank.
        $1\frac{1}{2}$,, ,, ,, Captains and Commanders } and officers of corresponding
        $1\frac{1}{4}$,, ,, ,, Lieutenants ... ...} ranks.

Plain.—
    The same as the above, but no gold lace.

White.—
    Material.—Duck or drill.

10.—WAISTCOATS. (Plate VIII.)

Morning.

For all Officers.—Blue cloth, single breasted, with 6 buttons.

Evening.

Blue.—
    Blue cloth, single breasted, cut low, with 4 buttons; a gold braid edging down the front, and along the bottom to the side seam, the pocket edged with a similar braid. The braid to be $\frac{1}{8}$ inch wide.

For Warrant Officers.—The same, but without gold braid.

White.—
    White marcella, the same pattern as the blue waistcoat.

11.—EPAULETTES. (Plates XIV. and XV.)

For convenience in describing the epaulette, reference is made to its several parts, viz.:—the strap, the crescent, the bullion, and the devices.

Strap.

For Admiral of the Fleet.—Gold lace, embroidered with gold oak leaf and acorns, with pearl crescent and edging of gold.

For all other Commissioned Officers of the Military Branch.—Plain gold lace, with pearl crescent and edging of gold.

For the Civil Branch.—Gold lace, but the edging to be of silver, $\frac{1}{8}$ of an inch wide, continued round inside the crescent, and outside below it.

Gold Bullions. (Plate XII.)

Officers of Flag Rank.—A double row of loose dead and bright bullions, 3 inches deep; the outer row to have 20 bullions, $1\frac{3}{8}$ inch in circumference; the inner row to have 19 bullions, $1\frac{1}{4}$ inch in circumference.

Commodores, and Captains.—A double row of bright bullions, 3 inches deep; the outer row to have 22 bullions, $1\frac{1}{4}$ inch in circumference; the inner row to have 21 bullions, $1\frac{1}{8}$ inch in circumference.

Commanders, and Lieutenants.—A double row of bright bullions, $2\frac{3}{4}$ inches deep; the outer row to have 20 bullions, $1\frac{1}{8}$ inch in circumference; the inner row to have 19 bullions, $\frac{7}{8}$ inch in circumference.

Sub-Lieutenants, and Officers of corresponding rank. Epaulette straps only—no bullions.

Officers of the Civil Branch, the same according to relative rank.

See Tailor Pattern **F**, *Page* 29.

Devices. (Plate XVI.)

The devices are:—Crowns; crossed batons in a wreath of laurel; crossed baton and sword; stars of two sizes, large* and small, the former 2 inches, the latter $1\frac{1}{4}$ inch in diameter; anchor and chain cable; and crossed anchors. The devices for the Military Branch are in silver; those for the Civil Branch, in gold, picked out with silver. To be placed on the strap according to pattern.

The Epaulette devices of the several ranks are as follows:—

Admiral of the Fleet.—A crown, crossed batons surrounded by a wreath of laurel.

Admiral.—A crown, cross sword and baton, three stars.

Vice-Admiral.—A crown, crossed sword and baton, two stars.

Rear-Admiral.—A crown, crossed sword and baton, one large star.

Commodores, and Captains over 3 years' seniority.—A crown, two stars, an anchor and chain cable.

---

* For Rear-Admirals, and Inspectors-General of Hospitals and Fleets.

Captain under 3 years' seniority.—A crown, one star, an anchor and chain cable.

Commander.—A crown, an anchor and chain cable.

Lieutenant over 8 years' seniority.—One star, an anchor and chain cable.

Lieutenant under 8 years' seniority, and Sub-Lieutenant.—An anchor and chain cable.

Officers of the Navigating Branch will wear crossed anchors without cables instead of the anchor and chain cable; in other respects the devices will be the same as the above, according to rank.

Inspector-General of Hospitals and Fleets.—A crown, one small star, and a large star.

Other Officers of the Civil Branch.—The same devices as the corresponding ranks in the Military Branch, except that a star will be worn instead of the anchor and chain cable.

12.—SHOULDER STRAPS. (PLATES XVII. AND XVIII.)

FOR GREAT COAT, WHITE UNDRESS, AND WHITE JACKET.

For Flag Officers, and Commodores, 1st Class.—Blue cloth; the top covered with 2-inch wide gold lace, showing a margin of $\frac{1}{4}$ of an inch of cloth; the same devices as on the epaulettes, but the large star to be $1\frac{3}{4}$ inch, and the small stars 1 inch in diameter.

For all other Commissioned Officers.—Blue cloth, with distinction lace, and coloured cloth, according to rank and branch, the same as worn on the sleeves of the frock coat.

For Warrant Officers.—Blue cloth, with distinction lace according to rank and branch for officers over 10 years' seniority, and plain for others.

Shoulder straps to be $5\frac{1}{4}$ inches long, $2\frac{1}{4}$ inches wide, and to have a button at the top.

The method of attachment to coats to be in accordance with sealed patterns.

13.—BUTTONS. (PLATE XII.)

Buttons are of two patterns—A and B.
- A. For Officers of Flag Rank.
- B. " all other Officers.

PATTERN A.

A gilt-raised round button with a rope rim encircling a plain rim, inside of which is a wreath of laurel surrounding an anchor and cable under a crown.

PATTERN B.

The same as A, but no laurel wreath.

Buttons are of three sizes—

1. $\frac{7}{8}$ of an inch in diameter (or in button maker's measure 35 lines ; relief, 7 lines).
2. $\frac{13}{16}$ „ „ { „ „ „ 30 „ „ 6 „ }.
3. $\frac{5}{8}$ „ „ { „ „ „ 25 „ „ $5\frac{1}{4}$ „ }.

They are to be worn as follows :—
    Size No. 1. On all Coats and Cocked Hats.
    „ „ 2. On Jackets, and Slashes of Full Dress Coats.
    „ „ 3. On Waistcoats, Epaulettes, and Shoulder Straps.

14.—SWORDS. (PLATE XIX.)

For all Officers other than as specified below.—Gilt mounted, the hilt solid half basket guard, with raised bars, and crown and anchor badge, lion head back-piece, white fish skin gripe, bound with three gilt wires ; outside length $5\frac{3}{4}$ inches, inside length $4\frac{1}{2}$ inches. The blade slightly curved, $31\frac{1}{4}$ inches long, $1\frac{1}{8}$ inch wide at the shoulder, with a flat back, and the blade ground hollow to within 11 inches of the end, with a double-edged spear point.

For Chief Gunners, Boatswains, and Carpenters, and Warrant Officers.—The same as above, except that the back piece of the handle is to be plain, with a flute round the top and down the back, with a black fish-skin gripe bound with three gold threads.

Assistant Clerks.—No sword or dirk.

SCABBARDS. (PLATE XIX.)

For Flag Officers, and Commodores.—Black leather, the top and middle lockets to be 4 and $3\frac{1}{2}$ inches long respectively ; to have loops and rings, and to be ornamented with embossed oak leaves in bas-relief ; the chape to be $7\frac{1}{2}$ inches long, and to have oak leaves, as above, round the upper part, and a honeysuckle ornament at the end.

For all other Officers.—The chape to be only $6\frac{1}{2}$ inches long ; both lockets and chape to be ornamented with fluted threads and scrolls, instead of oak leaves.

SWORD KNOT. (PLATE XIX.)

For all Officers.—Of blue and gold cord with barrel-shaped mould covered with blue and gold gimp, with blue bullion at end.

DIRK. (PLATE XIX.)

For Midshipmen and Naval Cadets.—Gilt mounted, with white fish skin grip ; hilt $5\frac{1}{2}$ inches long, the cross bar fitted with an oval medallion with crown and anchor badge surrounded by a wreath of laurel, and with spring to hold the blade to the scabbard ; blue and gold blade, embossed, $17\frac{3}{4}$ inches long ; length of dirk when in the scabbard, $23\frac{1}{4}$ inches.

Scabbard.—Black leather, 18 inches long, fitted with gilt locket at the top, with two rings to attach to slings of belt, and bottom a gilt pointed shoe.

Knot.—The same as for swords, but smaller.

Belt.—The same as Lieutenant's undress belt, but with short slings.

15.—FULL DRESS SWORD BELTS. (Plate XX.)

For Flag Officers, and Commodores.—Black morocco leather, lined, girdle fully 1½ inch wide; slings 1 inch wide, on D's; the whole embroidered in gold, with oak leaves and acorns down the middle, and margined with a straight gold line near each edge. Gilt mountings with circular clasp in front, laurel embossed edges, crown, anchor, and laurel in the centre; embossed carriage buckles, plain side buckle, and a plain gilt hook, attached to the front D, to suspend the sword short. Swivels and buckles and billets to attach the sword.

For Captains, and Commanders.—The same as for Flag Officers, except:—girdle and slings to be embroidered with three straight gold lines, one down the middle and one at each margin near the edge; the circular clasp to have embossed laurel edges, crown and anchor in the centre; plain carriage and side buckles.

For Lieutenants, Sub-Lieutenants.—The same, but two lines of gold embroidery instead of three.

For Officers of the Civil Branch.—The same as the above, according to relative rank.

For Chief Gunners, Boatswains, and Carpenters, and Warrant Officers.—The same as Sub-Lieutenants in undress.

Undress Sword Belts. (Plate XX.)

For all Officers.—The same as full dress, but no embroidery. Slings to be ⅜ inch wide.

16.—AIGUILLETTES. (Plate VI.)

For Admiral of the Fleet.—Is of gold wire basket cord, ¼ of an inch thick, and consists of two single plaits of cord and two cord loops, starting from each end of plait; at the termination of the plaits there are a few inches of plain cord ending in netted heads and gilt embossed metal tags. The plait and cord are joined together with blue cloth about 1½ inch wide, in which is a button-hole to allow of the aiguillette being fastened to the brass slide of the epaulette. The long cord is looped up on the top or front cord, the front cord and short and long plaits are fastened together, and a small gold braid loop is fixed thereon to attach to the top button on the right breast of coat. The aiguillette is worn on the *right* shoulder, the arm being passed through between front plait and cord, and the back or long plait and cord.

For Aides de Camp to the Queen.—*Dress.*—The same as for Admiral of the Fleet, except that gold gimp cord 1⅜ of an inch in diameter is used, instead of wire basket cord ¼ of an inch thick.

Undress.—As above, but of cord, 1⅛ of an inch thick, and fitted with plaited shoulder strap, it is fastened to the coat in a similar manner to the epaulette.

For Captain of the Fleet, Chief of Staff, Flag Captains, Flag Lieutenants, and Secretaries to Flag Officers and Commodores.—Is of similar pattern to that for Aide de Camp to the Queen, but is made of gold and blue cord ⅗ of an inch thick; and the gilt metal tags are of special design, mounted with silver metal anchors. The aiguillette is attached to the coat by a blue cloth shoulder strap, and fastened to it in a similar manner to that of an epaulette.

Note.—The aiguillette to be fastened to the top button on the same side of the coat as that upon which it is worn. This applies to all coats.

Sash. (Plate VI.)

For Honorary Physicians and Surgeons to the Queen.—Gold net sash, 3 inches wide, with two black stripes, $\frac{3}{8}$ of an inch wide, gold netted slides and netted gimp heads, with gold fringe tassels.

17.—COCKED HAT. (Plate XXI.)

For convenience, the hat and device are described separately. The hat is a black cocked hat with a left flap of 6 inches, right of $5\frac{1}{2}$ inches, $4\frac{1}{2}$ inches at each corner ; *for Flag Officers and Commodores,* bound all round with gold lace two inches wide, showing one inch on each side : and *for all other officers (Subordinate officers excepted)* bound with black silk of the oak-leaf and acorn pattern, $1\frac{3}{4}$ inches wide, showing 1 inch on the outer side. A black silk cockade, 5 inches wide, placed upright. A tassel at each end consisting of five gold bullions above five gold and five blue bullion-eyes.

Devices. (Plate XXI.)

For Flag Officers and Commodores, on the Cockade.—Three loops of dead and bright bullion, $1\frac{1}{2}$ inch in circumference, the centre loop to be twisted, and looped round a button.

For Captains and Commanders.—Two loops of bright bullion. $1\frac{1}{2}$ inch in circumference, the inner loop to be twisted, and looped round a button.

For Lieutenant, Sub-Lieutenant, Chief Gunner, and Chief Boatswain.—The same, but only one twisted loop.

For Warrant Officers.—No device.

For Officers of the Civil Branch.—The same as for the Military Branch, except that the loops are of $\frac{1}{2}$-inch gold lace instead of bullion, the centre loop not twisted.

18.—CAP AND COVER. (Plate XXII.)

For all Officers.—Blue cloth, with three blue cloth welts, $3\frac{1}{4}$ inches total depth, diameter across the top $8\frac{1}{4}$ inches for a cap fitting $21\frac{3}{4}$ inches in circumference, the top to be $\frac{1}{4}$ inch larger or smaller in diameter for every $\frac{1}{4}$ inch the cap may vary in size of head above or below the before-mentioned standard, *i.e.*, a cap $22\frac{1}{4}$ inches in circumference, diameter across the top $8\frac{1}{2}$; cap 21 inches in circumference, diameter $7\frac{7}{8}$. The sides to be made in four pieces, and to be $1\frac{1}{2}$ inch deep between the welts ; a black mohair braid band $1\frac{1}{2}$ wide placed between the two lower welts, the join of the band to be in front so as to be covered by the badge, the upper edge of the mohair band to be left unsewn to admit of bottom edge of white cover being slipped under, when required.

The cap set up on a band of stiff leather, or other material, $1\frac{3}{4}$ inches deep.

Cover.—The cap cover to be of white ribbed marcella.

Peak. (Plate XXIII.)

For Flag Officers.—Covered with blue cloth and bound with patent leather, and embroidered all round with oak leaves in gold $\frac{3}{4}$ of an inch wide.

For Captains and Commanders.—The same, but embroidered on the front edge only.

For Inspectors-General of Hospitals and Fleets.—The same as for Flag Officers, except that a band, ⅝ of an inch wide, embroidered in gold, is to be substituted for the oak leaf embroidery.

For Officers of the Civil Branch of corresponding ranks to Captain and Commander.—The same as for Captains, but a band, ¾ of an inch wide, embroidered in gold, substituted for the oak leaf embroidery.

For all other Officers.—Patent leather, without embroidery.

The peak to droop at an angle of 45 degrees, and to be 2 inches deep in the middle when worn with embroidery, and 1¾ inch when plain.

Chin stay for all Officers.—Black patent leather ¾ inch wide, buttoned on to two japanned buttons placed immediately behind the corners of the peak.

19.—CAP BADGES. (Plate XXII.)

Military Branch.—A wreath of gold laurel leaves surrounding a silver foul anchor, embroidered on a blue cloth ground, with a Crown above it embroidered in gold and silver.

For Commissioned and Warrant Officers.—The outside dimensions of the badge to be 2½ inches high by 3 inches broad ; *for Subordinate Officers*, 1¾ inches by 2¾ inches.

For the Civil Branch.—The same badge, but in gold only.

20.—HELMET. (Plate XXII.)

For all Officers.—Made of cork, covered with white jean, and bound with thin buff leather, with ventilating button at top, the peak being sufficiently spread out to afford ample protection from the sun ; between the interior head piece and the body of helmet is a space to allow of ventilation. A brown leather chin stay ¾ of an inch wide, with a gilt slide. A white cotton puggaree, folded back and front, with dark blue silk about ¼ inch wide showing at top edge.

21.—FOUL WEATHER HAT. (Plate XXII.)

A black Sou'wester of the usual pattern.

22.—NECKTIES AND COMFORTER.

Neckties :—

With frock coats or undress.—A plain black silk or satin tie, 1½ to 2 inches wide.

With ball dress, mess dress, and mess undress.—A plain black silk or satin tie, 1 inch wide.

Comforter, to be white.

23.—GLOVES.

Plain, white.

Plain, brown dogskin, or brown buckskin.

24.—BOOTS.

Black.—Plain-fronted Wellingtons or false Wellingtons.

    Lace-up boots or lace-up shoes. No toe caps.

White.—Lace-up white buckskin shoes. No toe caps, or straps.

25.—GAITERS. (Plate XXII.)

Black grain hide, with four eyelet holes each side, and fastened with leather loops, strap and buckle at the top, the strap to go completely round the gaiter. To be 10 inches high.

26.—GREAT COAT. (Plate VII.)

For all Officers.—To be worn over full dress and other uniform. Blue cloth. Length to come to 14 inches from the ground. Double breasted. Six buttons on each side, the bottom button not to come below the level of hips. A plait down the back, with an opening at the bottom 18 inches long with a fly and four small plain buttons. A cloth strap behind with a button-hole at each end 8 inches apart, and two corresponding uniform buttons to confine the waist to required size. Stand and fall collar with hook and eye in collar seam. Edges of coat to be double stitched; the shoulders fitted with straps (if required).

Sword, when worn with the great coat, is to be hooked up, the scabbard passing through a slit in the coat, and the hilt outside.

27.—WATERPROOF COAT AND CAPE. (Plate VII.)

To be of the shape and colour (dark blue) of the Admiralty pattern. Material optional. The cape of the waterproof may be worn by itself.

28.—BOAT CLOAK. (Plate VII.)

The same shape as the waterproof, but without sleeves. Blue cloth, the cape lined with white, and the coat lined with black.

NOTE.—The use of the boat cloak is optional, if worn it is to be restricted solely to boat service, other than drills and exercises, and evening wear.

DRESS OF CHAPLAINS.

On board his ship, and on all occasions when the officers of the ship are ordered to appear in uniform, a Chaplain shall wear a clerical collar or stock or a collar and white tie, and shall be dressed in other respects in such a manner as shall clearly indicate his profession.

On all occasions when officers are required to appear in frock coats, the Chaplain's dress shall be a black cloth frock coat and waistcoat, and trousers which are either black or of a dark mixture.

A Chaplain shall also wear on board his ship a black clerical felt hat or college cap; and when attending on shore with officers in uniform, he shall wear either the former or a tall black silk hat.

A Chaplain's ordinary mess dress shall be a clerical court coat, a waistcoat, and trousers, all of black cloth; but, in the evening, when officers wear full dress, or ball dress, the waistcoat shall be a black silk cassock one, and, instead of trousers, shall be worn black cloth knee breeches, with black silk stockings and patent leather shoes with silver or plated buckles.

When white dress is worn by officers, a Chaplain may (if he please) wear a plain white tunic and white trousers; and in that case he shall wear either a service pattern white helmet with white puggaree, or a white or black and white straw hat with black ribbon.

When white jackets are worn at mess, he shall wear a white jacket.

UNIFORM FOR OFFICERS OF ROYAL NAVAL RESERVE.

(23.) Officers of the Royal Naval Reserve are to wear the same uniform as officers of corresponding rank in the Royal Navy, with the following exceptions, viz. :—Instead of each stripe of half-inch lace round the sleeves of the coat, there is to be a stripe formed of two waved lines of quarter-inch gold braid, intersecting each other, so as to form bands half an inch wide, the blue cloth to show between the curves.

(24.) The buttons to be of the Royal Navy pattern, with the letters " R.N.R." in Old English character, across the anchor.

(25.) Instead of the anchor on the epaulettes and shoulder straps respectively, there is to be a badge consisting of a silver anchor in the centre, surrounded with the words " Royal Naval Reserve " embroidered in gold.

(26.) Instead of the bullion loop on the cocked hats, the loop to be formed of two gold braids, twisted the same as for coat sleeves.

(27.) *Badge for the Cap.*—A silver anchor, with the letters " R.N.R." above it in gold, on a medallion of black velvet, encircled by an edging of gold lace, surrounded by a laurel wreath of gold embroidery, except at the top, where a crown, embroidered in gold and silver with a crimson velvet centre, is to be placed over the medallion.

(28.) The plate for the sword-belt to be the same as for officers of the Royal Navy, with the letters " R.N.R." across the anchor.

(29.) The Engineers' department are to be distinguished by purple velvet stripes, quarter inch wide, between the gold braid waved lines round the sleeves of the coat.

(30.) The Paymasters' department are to be distinguished by white velvet stripes, quarter inch wide, between the gold braid waved lines round the sleeves of the coat.

(31.) Assistant Paymasters are to wear immediately below the one waved line of gold braid round the sleeve of the coat a stripe of quarter inch white velvet.

(32.) Midshipmen are to wear a double-breasted jacket of blue cloth, with the R.N.R. buttons on the breast and cuffs, each row of buttons to consist of nine, placed in threes. Distinctive marks at each end of the collar to be a button-hole of blue twist with R.N.R. buttons. Trousers to be of blue cloth ; waistcoat to be of white or blue cloth, or kerseymere, single breasted, with small R.N.R. buttons ; cap, the ordinary uniform cap with the R.N.R. badge ; a sword is to be worn when appointed to a ship for a year's training, but Midshipmen will not be required to wear a sword when appointed to H.M. ships for short periods or when on drill.

UNIFORM FOR ROYAL INDIAN MARINE.

The uniform is to be the same as that authorised for the Royal Naval Reserve, except that the letters R.I.M. are to be substituted on epaulettes, shoulder straps, cap badges, buttons, &c., for the words " Royal Naval Reserve," and the letters R.N.R., as the case may be, wherever they occur.

GENERAL INSTRUCTIONS.

Article of Uniform, &c.	Instructions.
*Aiguillettes, for Admirals of the Fleet, and Aides de Camp to the Queen.	To be worn on the right shoulder with full and other dresses (jacket excepted), when in attendance on the Sovereign or on the Royal Family; also on occasions of ceremony, although not in attendance.
*Aiguillette for Officers of Admiral's and Commodore's, Staff.	To be worn on the left shoulder with all dresses by the Captain of the Fleet, Chief of Staff, Flag-Captain, Secretary, and Flag-Lieutenant. The aiguillette need not be worn at sea.
Boots and shoes ...	Boots with plain fronts to be worn with—
	Full dress.
	Ball dress.
	Frock coat with epaulettes dress, and
	Mess dress.
	Lace-up boots by officers with landing parties.
	Boots of either description, or lace-up shoes, on other occasions.
Coats ...	To be worn buttoned, viz. :—
	Full dress, to button all buttons. Collar hooked.
	Frock coat ,, 4 lower buttons.
	Undress coat ,, 4 ,, ,,
	White undress coat to button all buttons. Collar hooked.
	Undress tail coat, when worn for full dress purposes by Midshipmen and Clerks, to button 4 lower buttons.
Gloves ...	White gloves are to be worn with full, ball, and frock coat with epaulettes, dresses.
	If worn with other dresses, except undress, the gloves to be white.
	If worn with blue or white undress, the gloves to be brown dogskin or brown buckskin, but in cold weather white knitted gloves may be worn.
	If worn on occasions when the white undress is authorised in lieu of No. 3 or No. 4 dress, the gloves are to be white.
Jewellery ...	Watch chains, and trinkets, are not to be worn outside coats; nor pins, rings, or other ornaments, on neckties.
Material of blue uniform ...	To be of smooth cloth, thickness to vary according to climate. No silk facings. For cold weather pilot cloth is allowed.
	In hot climates, when white undress is worn, the material for night uniform (undress) may, at the option of the wearer, be fine blue serge or flannel, instead of cloth.
Mourning ...	On all occasions of mourning, officers are to wear a piece of black crape, 2½ inches wide round the left arm above the elbow, and no other mark of mourning is ever to be worn unless specially ordered.

* Not to be worn on the Great Coat.

GENERAL INSTRUCTIONS—continued.

Article of Uniform, &c.	Instructions.
Neckties	For ball dress, mess dress, and mess undress, the bow tie; on all other occasions, the sailor's knot.
Shirts and collars	To be white.
Sword belts	To be worn, over the full dress and frock coats, between the two lowest buttons; under the blue, and white, undress coats; and under the waistcoat when worn with ball dress.
White cap covers	To be worn with white trowsers. Whenever he considers it desirable, the senior officer present is also to direct that white cap covers be worn with plain blue trowsers.
White trowsers	To be worn at home and abroad by direction of the senior officer present. Officers and men are always to wear trowsers of the same colour; this rule, however, does not apply when the men are in working dress.
White uniform	The senior officer present is to direct that the following articles of dress are to be worn in hot climates:— (1) *Helmet.*—At courts-martial and funerals with "white undress"; also when necessary on account of exposure to the sun. (2) *White jacket.*—With "mess undress." NOTE.—The wearing of the white jacket with "mess dress" is only to be by special order of the senior officer present. (3) *White undress coat.*—In lieu of the "frock" and "(blue) undress" coats on the occasions prescribed. Not to be worn with blue trowsers. (4) *White shoes.*—On board, with white trowsers. White shoes are to be worn on shore at the discretion of the senior officer present, who will take into consideration the conditions of climate.
Subordinate Officers	*Midshipmen, Naval Cadets, and Assistant Clerks,* are to wear the jacket on the occasions prescribed for full dress, ball dress, and frock coat dresses. *Clerks,* are to wear the undress tail coat for full dress purposes. *Midshipmen over 18 years of age,* may, at their option, provide themselves with the undress tail coat, when it will be worn for full dress and ball dress purposes instead of the jacket.
Foreign Officers	Foreign Officers, who are permitted to serve in the Royal Navy, are to be allowed to wear the uniform of the rank in which they may be serving.

DRESSES AND OCCASIONS ON WHICH THEY ARE TO BE WORN.

NOTE.—The O indicates that the sword is not to be worn.

Numbers are assigned to the several dresses for convenience when referring to them by signal.

	Dresses.		Occasions.
No. 1	"Full"	Full dress coat Epaulettes Laced trowsers Cocked hat Sword Full dress belt. Decorations and medals.	(a) State occasions at home and abroad. (b) When receiving the Sovereign, or other Crowned Heads, at ports at home and abroad. (c) †At ceremonies or entertainments when the senior officer present considers it desirable to do special honour to the occasion.
*No. 2	"Ball"	Undress tail coat Epaulettes Laced trowsers White waistcoat Decorations, and ribbons of medals, or miniature decorations and medals.	At official or public balls, dinners, and evening receptions.
No. 3	"Frock coat, with epaulettes."	Frock coat Epaulettes Morning waistcoat Trowsers, plain blue or white Cocked hat Sword Undress belt Ribbons of decorations and medals Stars of orders.	(a) When receiving their Royal Highnesses the Prince and Princess of Wales; Heirs to Thrones, or other Members of the English and foreign of Royal Families; at ports at home and abroad. All mast-head flags being hoisted. (b) Courts martial. (c) Funerals. (d) Boarding foreign ships-of-war. (e) Exchanging visits of ceremony, with foreign officers or other foreign functionaries. (f) Occasions of duty and ceremony when the frock coat dress is not sufficient.

* Cocked hat, sword, and undress belt, may be ordered with this dress if desirable when meeting foreign officers (see general instructions, sword belts).
† To be worn by order of the senior officer present.

DRESSES AND OCCASIONS ON WHICH THEY ARE TO BE WORN—continued.

NOTE.—The O indicates that the sword is not to be worn.

	Dresses.		Occasions.
No. 4	"Frock coat"	Frock coat Morning waistcoat Trowsers, plain blue or white Cap Sword Undress belt Ribbons of decorations and medals.	(a) When receiving their Royal Highnesses the Prince and Princess of Wales; Heirs to Thrones, or other Members of the English and of foreign Royal Families; at ports at home and abroad. All mast-head flags not being hoisted. (b) Divisions on Sunday. (c) Inspections by Commander-in-Chief or Senior Officer. (d) Visit to Commander-in-Chief or Senior Officer. (e) Attending examinations, Surveys at hospitals. (f) Officer of the guard (exception, see No. 3 (d)). (g) Ordinary occasions of duty and ceremony on shore. O (h) Officers wearing uniform on leave in the daytime. Dances and entertainments, afloat or ashore, in the daytime. †Receptions in the daytime. O (i) Sunday in harbour, after divisions. O (j) Officer of the watch in harbour (Note —with sword belt.)
No. 5	"Undress"	Undress coat Morning waistcoat Trowsers, plain blue or white Cap Sword Undress belt Ribbons of decorations and medals.	(a) Drills,‡ exercises,‡ and occasions of duty afloat, other than those for which another dress is prescribed. (b) Patrol, dockyard duties, and landing parties. O (c) Officers at home ports going to and from their residences. O (d) On all other ordinary occasions afloat or in H.M. dockyards.

† Unless, the occasion requiring it, the Senior Officer present directs that swords be worn.
‡ The wearing, or not, of the sword must depend on the nature of the drill or exercise.

DRESSES AND OCCASIONS ON WHICH THEY ARE TO BE WORN—*continued.*

NOTE.—The O indicates that the sword is not to be worn.

	Dresses.		Occasions.
No. 6	"Mess Dress"	Jacket Evening waistcoat (blue) Laced trowsers Miniature decorations and medals, or ribbons of decorations and medals.	(a) Dinner in harbour at the tables of all Flag Officers, and Officers of corresponding rank, unless ball dress is ordered. (b) Evening dances and entertainments on shore or afloat. (c) Dinner at a military mess, and entertainments given by military Officers when they appear in their mess dress.
No. 7	"Mess Undress"	Jacket Evening waistcoat (blue) Plain blue trowsers Ribbons of decorations and medals, or ribbons of miniature decorations and medals.	(a) Dinner, at sea, at the tables of Flag Officers, and in harbour when guests are not entertained. (b) *Dinner at the tables of Captains or Officers in command. Ward-room and gun-room messes. (c) *Dinner at the messes of the Royal Naval Colleges, Barracks, and Medical Establishments.
	IN HOT CLIMATES.		
No. 8	"White Undress"	White undress coat Shoulder straps White trowsers Helmet or cap (white cover) Sword Undress belt.	(a) Occasions prescribed for No. 3 (b) and (c). *Note.— With Helmet.* (b) Occasions prescribed for No. 4 (b), (c), (d), (e), and (f). (c) †Occasions prescribed for No. 4 (g). (d) Occasions prescribed for No. 5 (a) and (b). O (e) Occasions prescribed for No. 4 (b), (i), and (j). O (f) Occasions prescribed for No. 5 (d).

* When Officers of Flag rank, or Military Officers of corresponding rank (wearing uniform) are guests, mess dress is to be worn.
NOTE.—Officers landing in the evening in uniform on ordinary leave are to wear their dinner dress (white jacket excepted).
† Unless, the occasion requiring it, No. 3 or No. 4 dress is ordered by the senior officer present.

27.

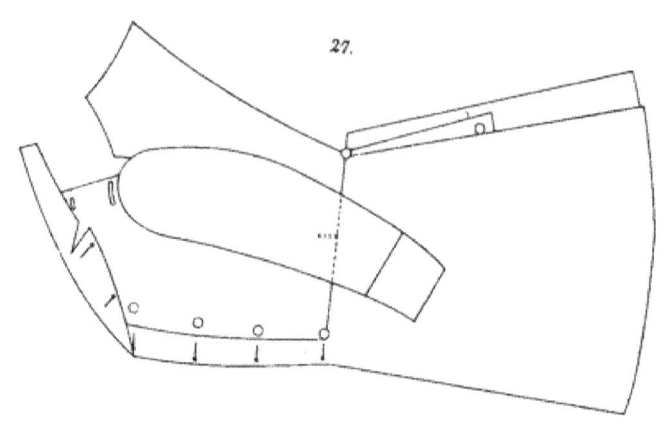

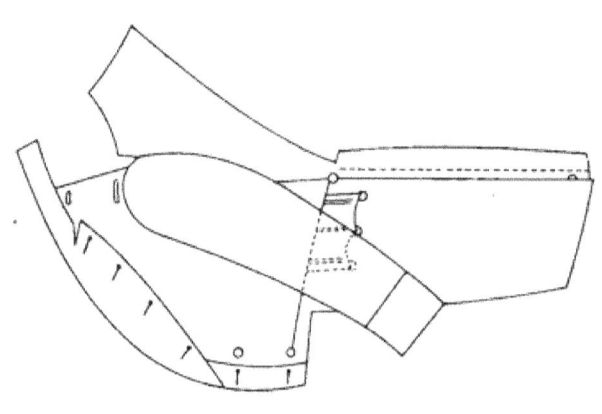

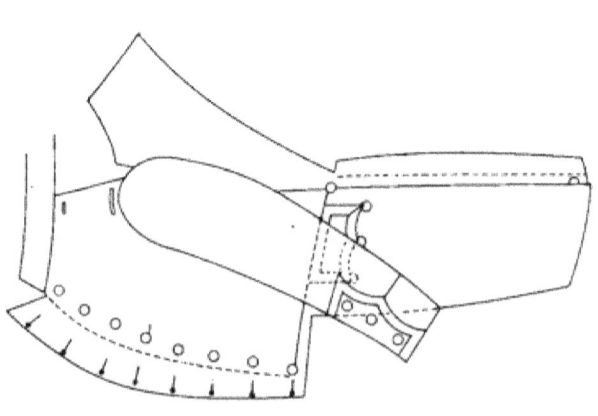

28.

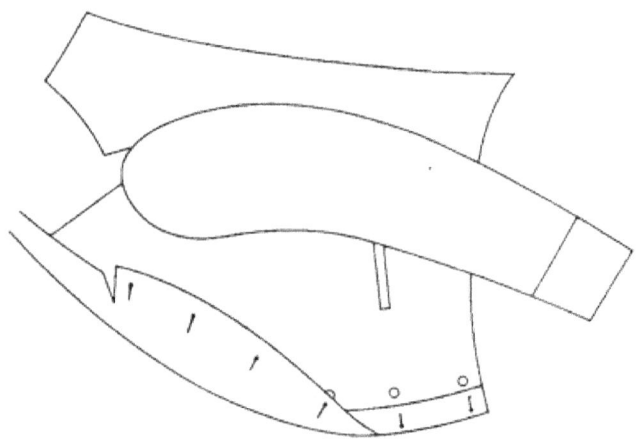

D. Undress Coat.

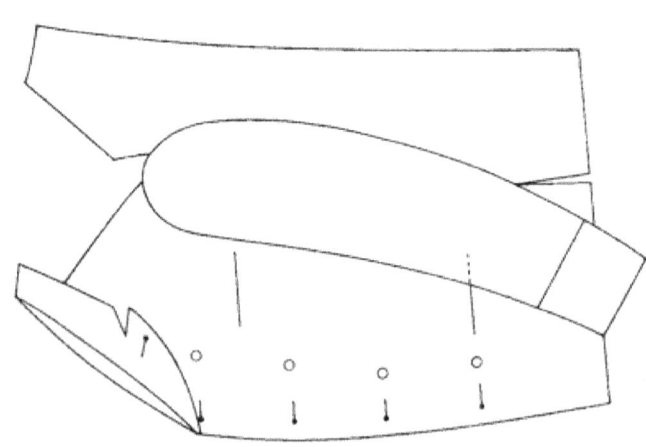

20.
F

ADMIRAL.
20 Dead and Bright Bullion.
3" long 1½ Inches in Circumference.
19 Back Bullion ⅝ in Circumference.

CAPTAIN.
22 Bright Bullion.
3" long 1½ Inches in Circumference.
21 Back Bullion ⅝ in Circumference.

LIEUTENANT & COMMANDER.
20 Bright Bullion.
2¼ Inches long 1½ in Circumference.
19 Back Bullion ⅝ in Circumference.

EPAULETTES.

PLAN. SHEWING THE NUMBER OF BULLION.

Nº 1. Full Dress.

Admiral of the Fleet.   Captain.

Nº 2. Ball Dress.

Admiral.   Lieutenant.

Plate III

Nº 3. Frock Coat with Epaulettes, Dress.
&
Nº 4. Frock Coat, Dress.

Commodore 2nd Class.   Flag Lieutenant.

Plate IV

Nº 5. Undress.

Captain.   Lieutenant (White Dress).

Plate V.

N° 6. Mess Dress
&
N° 7. Mess Undress.

Dress (Blue).   Undress (White).

Plate VI.

Aiguillette & Sash.

Captain
Aide-de-Camp to the Queen.

Inspector General of Hospitals.
Honorary Physician or Honorary Surgeon
to the Queen.

Plate VII.

Great Coat.

Waterproof. *Boat Cloak.*

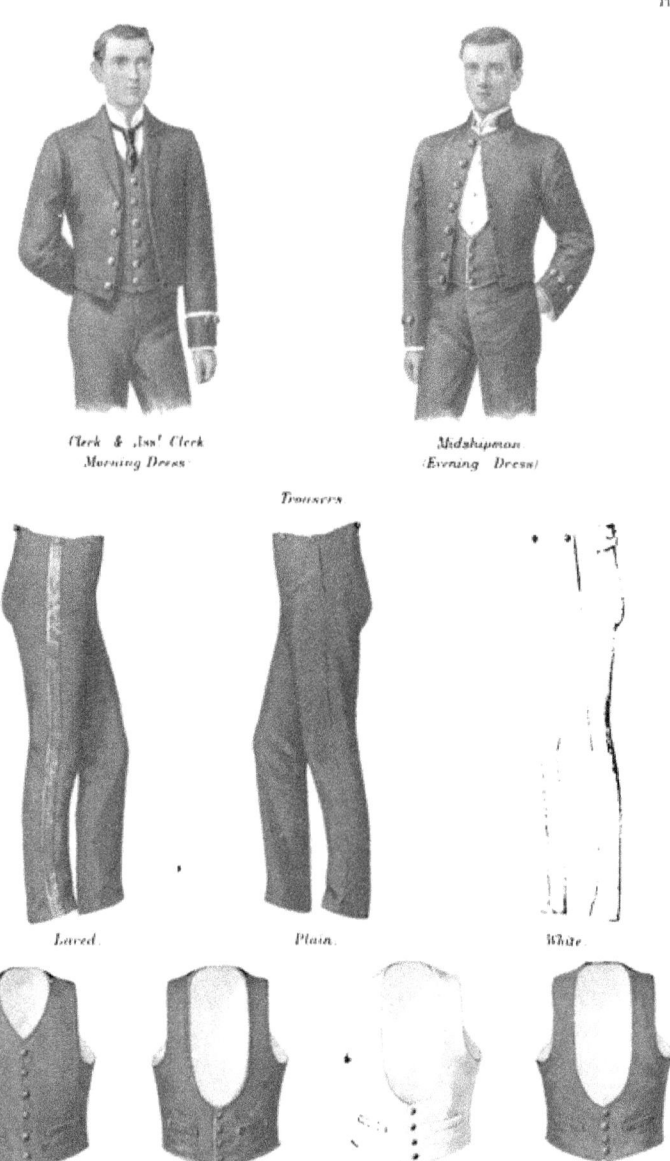

Plate VIII

Tail Coats Plate IX.

Flag Officers, Commodores
& Captains. Full Dress.

Commanders & Lieutenants.
Full Dress.

Undress Tail Coat
for all ranks.

Chief Gunner.
(Full Dress)

Chief Gunner.
Full Dress.

Plate X.

Sizes of Lace used.

2" - Flag Officer's Cocked Hat and Shoulder Strap.

1¾" - Flag Officer's Trowsers, Flaps on Shirt and band round Cuffs.

1½" - Flag Officer's Collars, Captain's and Commanders Trowsers and Flaps on Shirt.

1¼" - Captains & Commanders Collars and Lieutenants Trowsers.

1" - Flag Officers Slash on Sleeves.

1" - Lieutenants & Sub Lieutenants Collar & Flaps on Shirt.

¾" - Captains & Commanders Slash on Sleeves.

⅝" - Flag Officer's Collar and Stripes on Sleeve.

½" - Stripes on Sleeves & Shoulder Straps Collars of all Com'd Officers below Flag Rank. Slashes on Sleeve of Lieutenant & Sub Lieutenant.

¼" - Narrow Stripe on Sleeves & Shoulder Straps of Officers of rank of Lieut. over 8 years. and Warrant Officer over 10yrs service

1¾" - Black Lace for Cocked Hats of Officers below Flag Rank.

Plate XI

Collars for Full Dress.
(Full Size.)

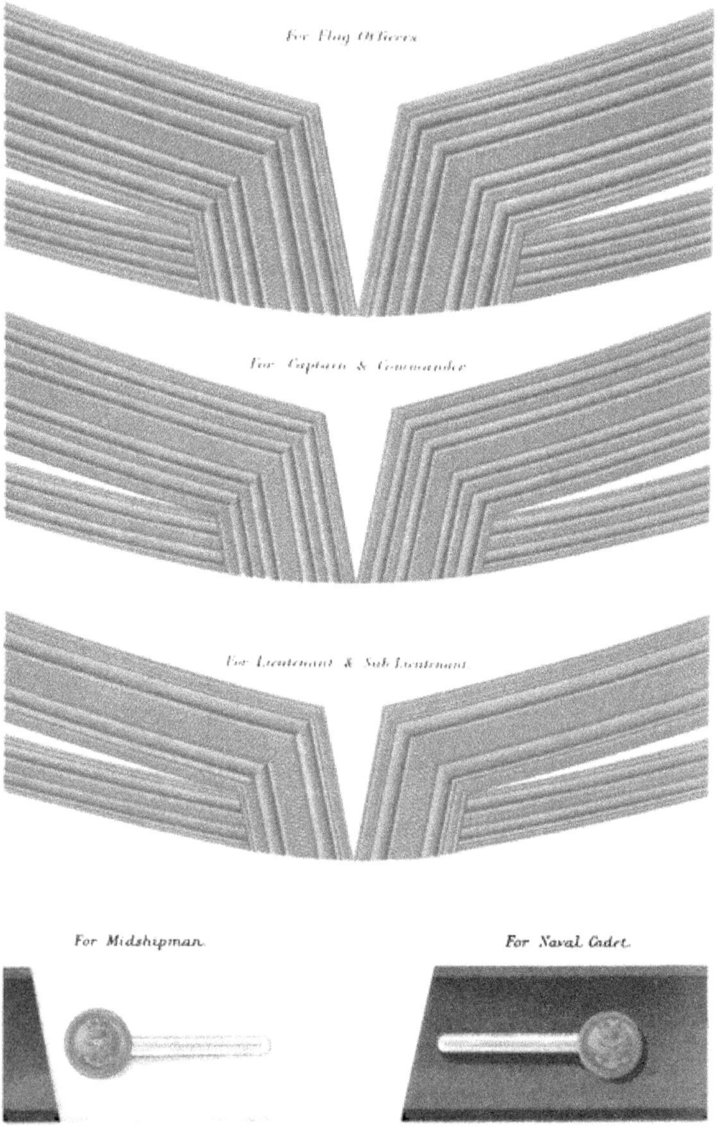

For Flag Officers.

For Captain & Commander.

For Lieutenant & Sub Lieutenant.

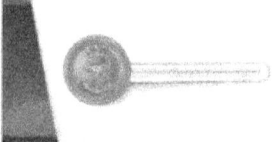

For Midshipman.

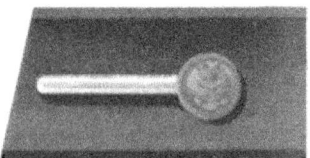

For Naval Cadet.

Plate XII

Cuffs of Full Dress Coats.
(Half Size)

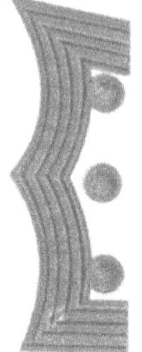

Flag Officer.

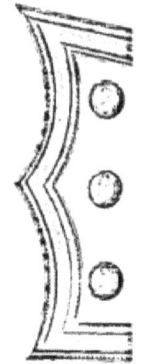

Captain & Commander.

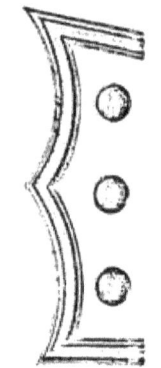

Lieutenant & Sub-Lieutenant.

Bullions.
(Full Size)

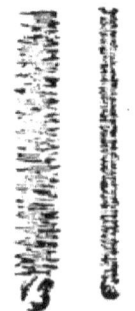

Flag Rank.

Captain.

Commander & Lieutenant and Officers of Corresponding Rank.

Buttons.
(Full Size)

Pattern A.

Flag Officers.

Pattern B.

all other Officers.

Cuffs (Full Dress)

Plate XIII

Military Branch		Medical	Civil Branches		Naval Instructors
			Accountant	Engineer	

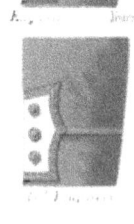
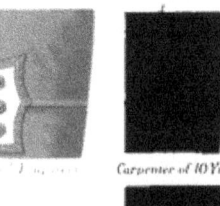
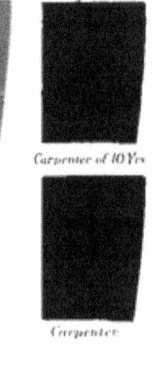

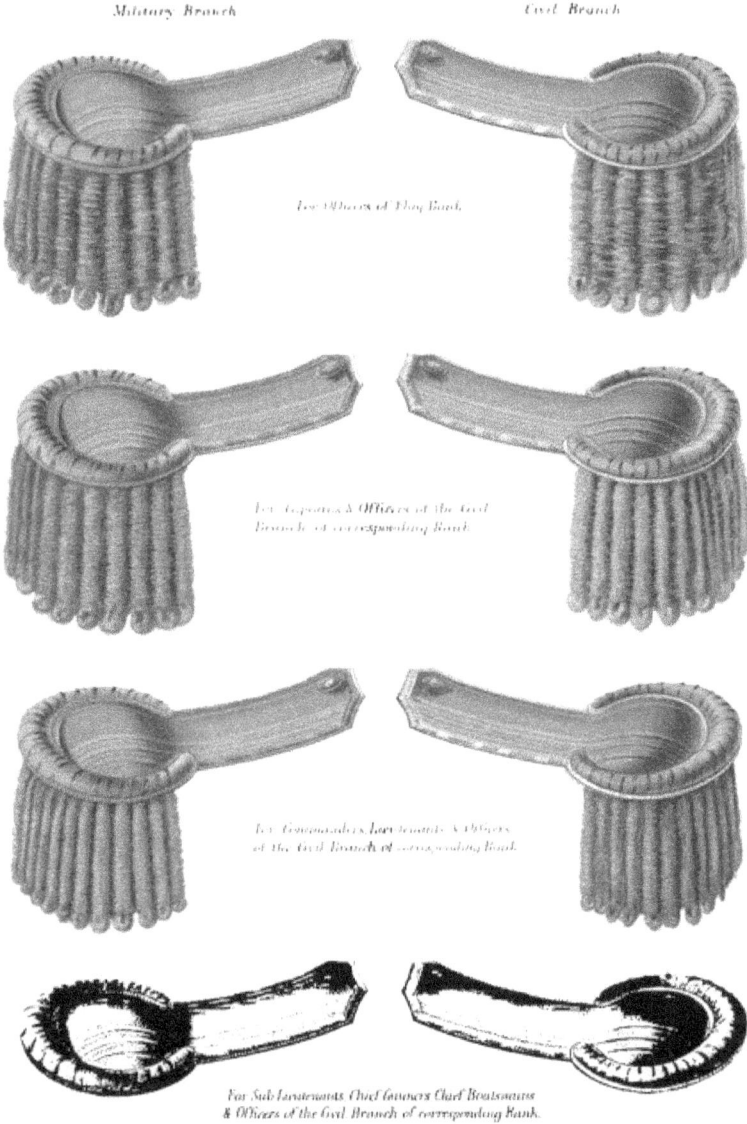

Epaulettes.

Epaulettes & Devices.

Plate XV.

Admiral of the Fleet.

Admiral.

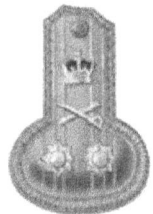
Vice Admiral.

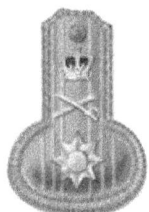
Rear Admiral.

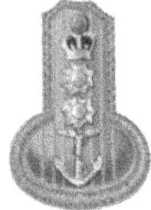
Commodore 2nd Class & Captain over 3 years' seniority.

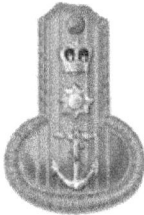
Captain under 3 years Seniority.

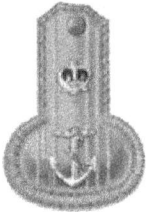
Commander.

Lieutenant over 8 years Seniority.

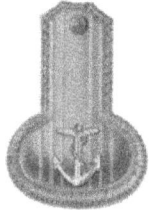
Lieutenant under 8 yrs. Seniority Sub Lieutenant Chief Gunner & Chief Boatswain.

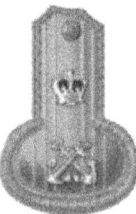
Staff Commander.

Inspector-General of Hospitals & Fleets.

Secretary to an Admiral of the Fleet.

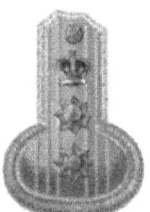
Inspector of Machinery under 8 years Service as such.

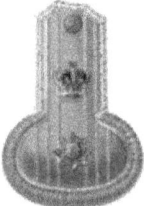
Fleet Surgeon.

Naval Instructor of 8 years Service.

Chief Carpenter.

Plate XVI

Epaulette Devices
(Full Size)

Admiral of the Fleet

Military Branch

Civil Branch

Admiral

Rear Admiral

Inspector-General of Hospitals & Fleets

Navigating Branch

Shoulder Straps. Nº 1. Plate XVII

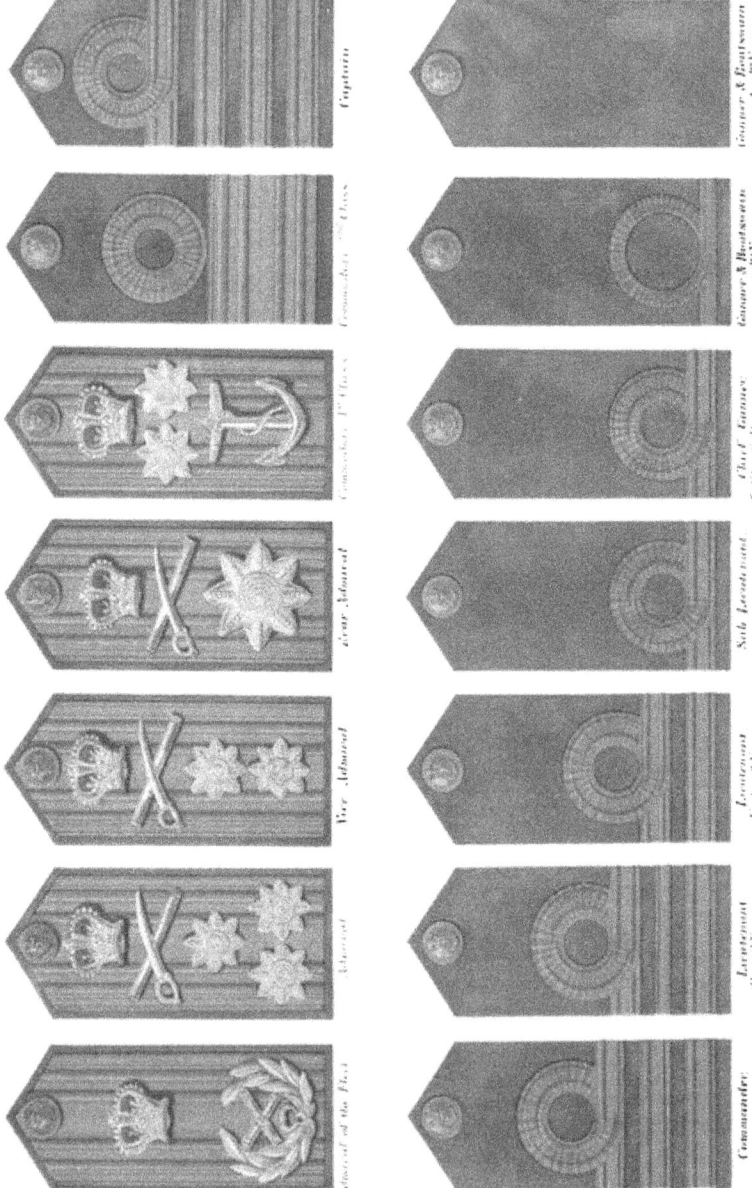

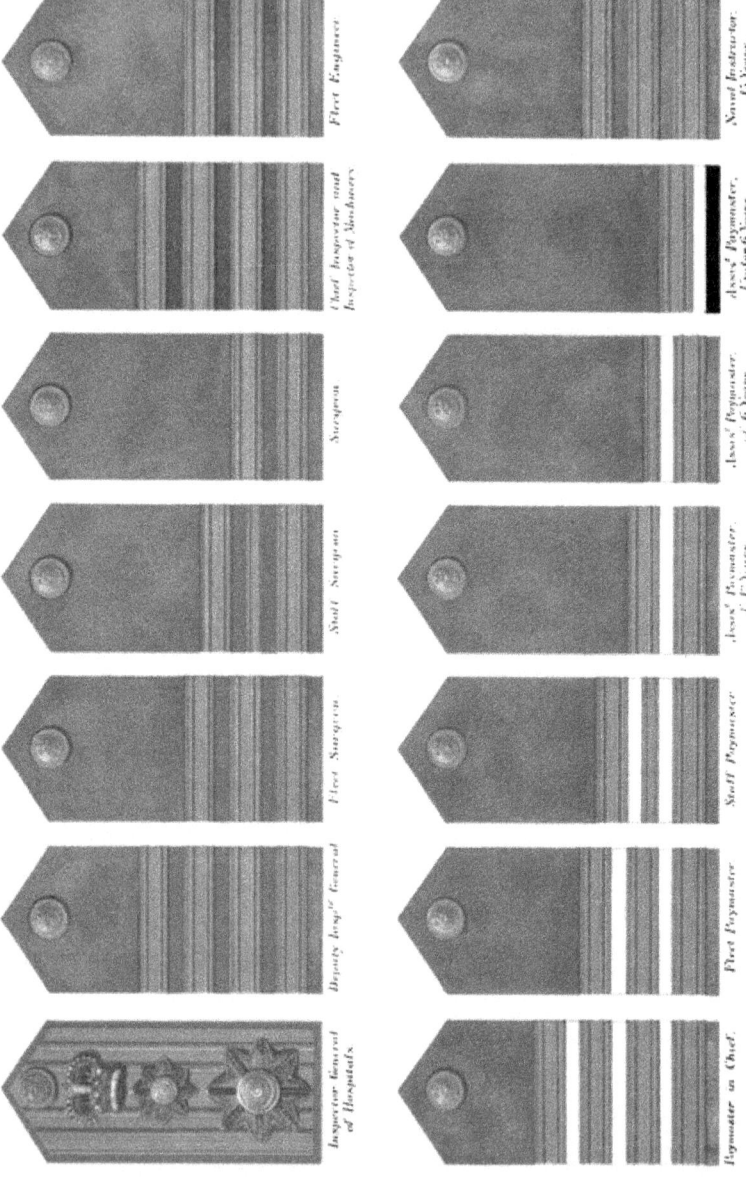

Plate XIX

Swords.

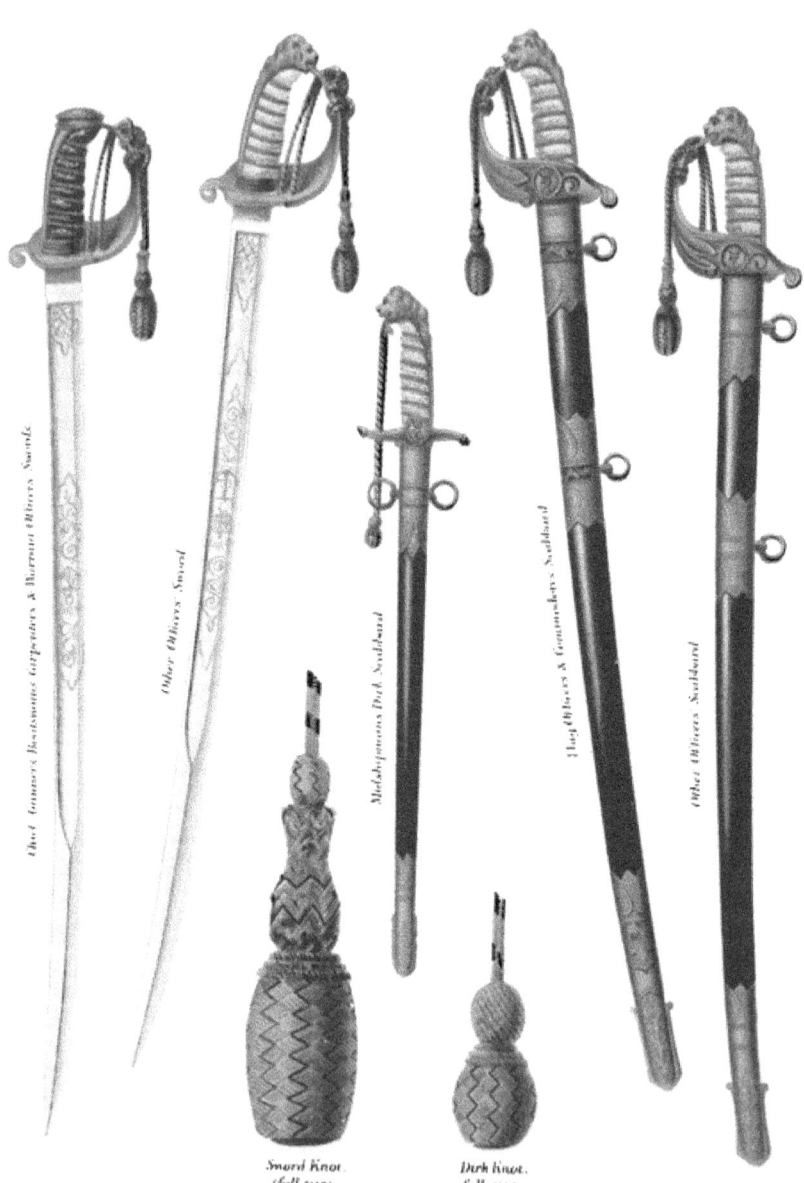

Sword Knot.
(full size)

Dirk knot.
full size

Plate XX.

Sword Belts.

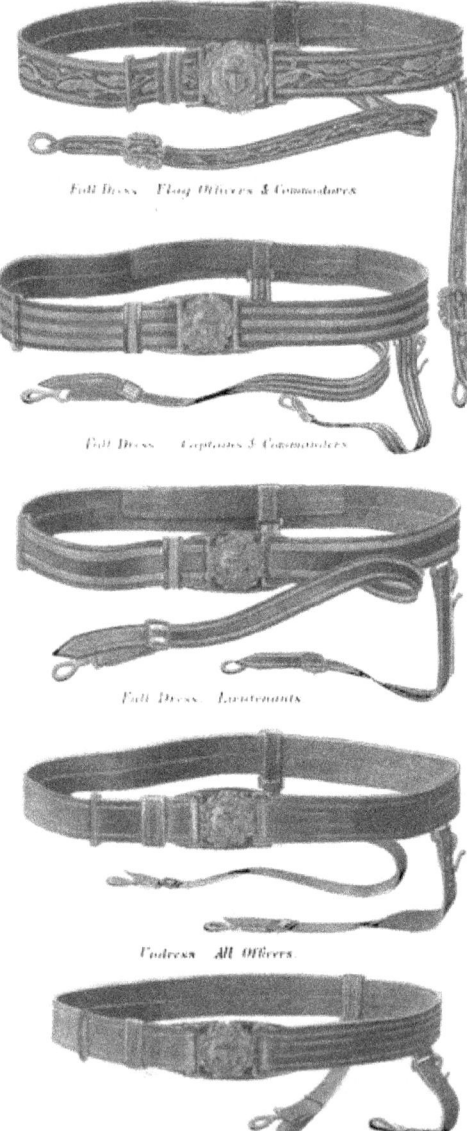

Full Dress. Flag Officers & Commodores.

Full Dress. Captains & Commanders.

Full Dress. Lieutenants.

Undress. All Officers.

Midshipmans Belt.

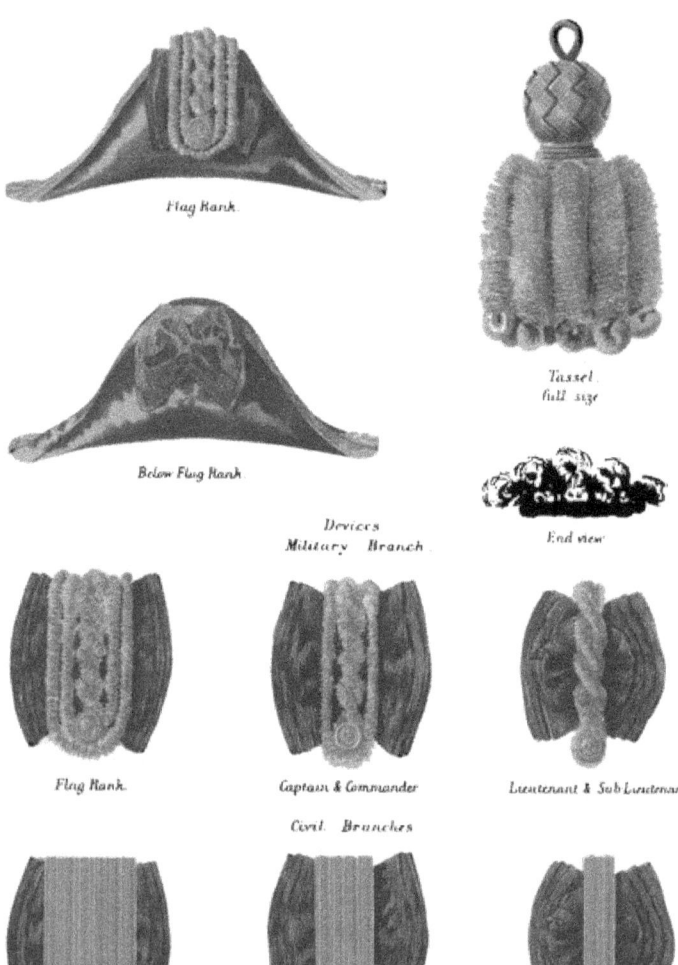

Plate XXI

Cocked Hats

Flag Rank.

Below Flag Rank.

Tassel full size

End view

Devices
Military Branch.

Flag Rank.   Captain & Commander   Lieutenant & Sub Lieutenant

Civil Branches

Caps, Badges, Helmet, &c. Plate XXII

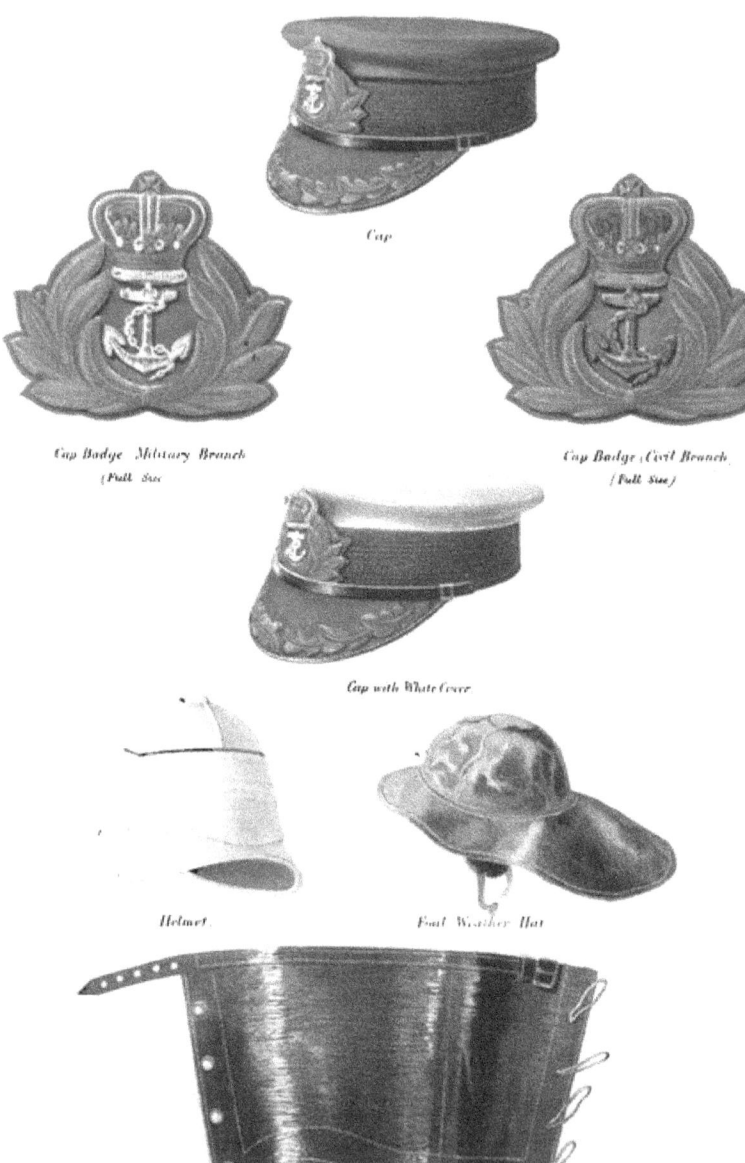

Cap Peaks
(½ Size)

Plate XXIII

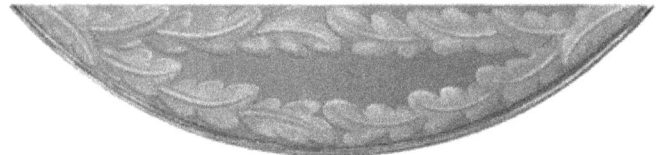

For Flag Officers

For Captains & Commanders

For Inspector General of Hospitals & Fleets

For Officers of Civil Branches,
Ranking with Captain & Commander

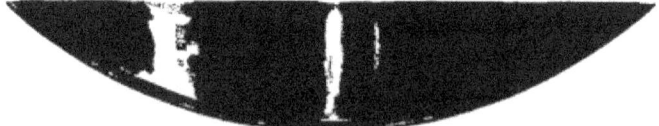

For all other Officers

Plate XXIV

Royal Naval Reserve.

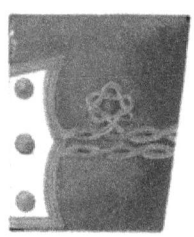

Military Branch.

Buttons.
(full size)

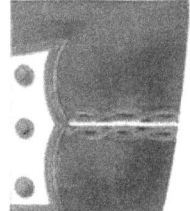

Civil Branch.

Epaulette Bosses for Military Branch
for Civil Branch all Gold
(full size)

Belt Plate.
(full size)

Cap Badge for Military Branch
for Civil Branch, all Gold.
(full size)

Shoulder Strap.

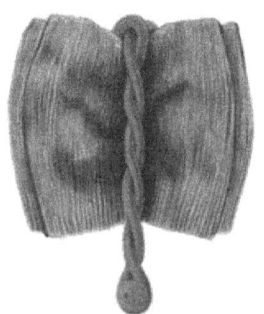

Cocked Hat Loop.
Military Branch.

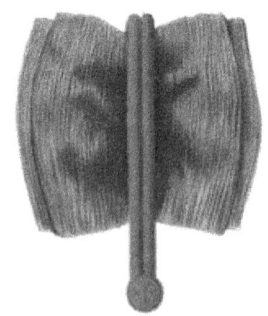

Cocked Hat Loop.
Civil Branch.

www.ingramcontent.com/pod-product-compliance
Lightning Source LLC
Chambersburg PA
CBHW020227090426
42735CB00010B/1612